SUPER-AWESOME SCIENCE

THE SCIENCE OF
SUPERHEROES

by Patricia Hutchison

Content Consultant
Suveen Mathaudhu, PhD
Assistant Professor, Materials Science and
Engineering
University of California Riverside

Core Library

An Imprint of Abdo Publishing
abdopublishing.com

abdopublishing.com

Published by Abdo Publishing, a division of ABDO, PO Box 398166, Minneapolis, Minnesota 55439. Copyright © 2017 by Abdo Consulting Group, Inc. International copyrights reserved in all countries. No part of this book may be reproduced in any form without written permission from the publisher. Core Library™ is a trademark and logo of Abdo Publishing.

Printed in the United States of America, North Mankato, Minnesota
042016
092016

Cover Photo: Columbia Pictures/Photofest
Interior Photos: Columbia Pictures/Photofest, 1, 4, 45; Walt Disney Studios Motion Pictures/ Photofest, 8, 43; Andrew Rich/iStockphoto, 10; Maltings Partnership © DK Images, 14; CBS/ Photofest, 16; DK Images, 19; Photos 12/Alamy, 20; © Walt Disney Studios Motion Pictures/ Everett Collection, 22, 32, 38; AF archive/Alamy, 24; © 20th Century Fox Film Corp. All rights reserved/Everett Collection, 26, 34; Twentieth Century Fox/Photofest, 30; iStockphoto, 36

Editor: Jon Westmark
Series Designer: Jake Nordby

Cataloging-in-Publication Data
Names: Hutchison, Patricia, author.
Title: The science of superheroes / by Patricia Hutchison.
Description: Minneapolis, MN : Abdo Publishing, [2017] | Series: Super-awesome
    science | Includes bibliographical references and index.
Identifiers: LCCN 2015960591 | ISBN 9781680782516 (lib. bdg.) |
    ISBN 9781680776621 (ebook)
Subjects: LCSH: Superheroes--Juvenile literature. | Heroes in literature--Juvenile
    literature. | Comic book characters--Juvenile literature.
Classification: DDC 741.5--dc23
LC record available at http://lccn.loc.gov/2015960591

CONTENTS

SUPERHEROES AND SCIENCE

A subway train speeds down the tracks, out of control. Spider-Man jumps in front, bracing his feet against the ties on the tracks. The wood splinters. The train keeps moving. The hero spreads himself out on the front of the train. He slings multiple webs from each hand that cling to the buildings on each side. The train begins to slow down. It finally comes to a stop, beyond the end of the tracks.

Superheroes' amazing feats often seem to defy the laws of physics.

The safe passengers are looking down at the river far below.

In this heart-pounding scene from *Spider-Man 2*, Spider-Man saves the day, stopping the train with his high-strength spiderwebs. Viewers may think this is just science fiction. Some physics students decided to do some tests to see if this scene could be real. The students calculated the force needed to stop the train. Next they studied the strength of a web created by a Darwin's bark spider. The students found that the superhero's silk could indeed have stopped the runaway train.

Part Fact, Part Fiction

Whether through reading a comic book or watching a movie, people are drawn to superhero stories. Often these stories are partly realistic and partly fantasy. Many show otherwise normal people doing extraordinary things. For example, in the Superman comic books, when he isn't wearing his superhero outfit, Superman looks like a normal person. But he is actually from a planet called Krypton. He has superpowers. He is much stronger and faster than people on Earth. Superman, the Hulk, Spider-Man, and many other superheroes possess special abilities ordinary people do not have. Others, such as Iron Man, are very intelligent and have highly developed technology.

Superheroes have unbelievable abilities, but many superhero abilities are based on real scientific ideas. Of course no one has actually come from the imaginary planet Krypton. No human naturally possesses

Science and Entertainment

The Science and Entertainment Exchange is a program of the National Academy of Sciences. Through this program, film and TV writers and producers gain easy access to top scientists and engineers. The scientists help writers create accurate storylines. They show that science is an exciting adventure. The Exchange helps filmmakers build new journeys that are based on real science. It helps bridge the gap between creative arts and the real world.

When Tony Stark is not in his Iron Man suit, he is an engineer.

Superman's ability to see through walls or fly. But science and technology allow humans to do these things. Superheroes bring these scientific ideas to life. Some are even scientists themselves.

Being Heroic

Superheroes use their powers to help others. They fight villains. They prevent natural disasters. They help people who are in trouble. Superheroes are able to do amazing works because they choose to use their abilities for good.

In the real world, humans have long used science to help others. People have used science to cure diseases, save people from disasters, learn about the universe, and much more. Studying science can help us learn how scientific principles shown in superhero stories operate in the real world.

EXPLORE ONLINE

Chapter One talks about the use of science in superhero stories. The website below goes into more detail about this subject. What information on the website is similar to the information in Chapter One? What new information did you learn from the website?

Spider-Math and Bat-Physics
mycorelibrary.com/science-of-superheroes

CHAPTER TWO

TESTING THE LAWS OF MOTION

Among their many skills, some superheroes have an ability to jump to amazing heights. An early version of Superman could leap to the top of tall buildings. The Hulk has jumped to the top of Mount Olympus, the highest mountain in Greece. How do they do it? Superheroes jump the same way ordinary humans do. The laws of motion, discovered by Isaac Newton in the late 1600s, help to explain

Superheroes jump the same as normal people. The difference is in the amount of force superheroes can exert.

how Superman, the Hulk, or anyone is able to jump.

A Giant Leap

The superhero stands on the sidewalk. Newton's first law of motion states, "A body at rest tends to stay at rest unless it is acted upon by an unbalanced force." A force is a push or pull on an object. If a superhero wants to leap a great height or distance, he or she must create a force to lift off the sidewalk.

In order to jump, the hero pushes down on the ground. This creates an unbalanced force.

Newton's third law of motion then comes into play. The third law states, "For every action, there is an equal and opposite reaction." The hero's feet push on the sidewalk, and the sidewalk pushes back with an equal force.

Newton's second law of motion has to do with speed: the more force applied to an object, the faster the object speeds up. Most humans can leap about two feet (0.6 m) in the air. To leap 660 feet (201 m), Superman must jump at a speed of 140 miles per hour (225 km/h). That means his legs must push on the sidewalk with 5,600 pounds (24,900 N) of force. In real life, the sidewalk would crumble under this amount of force.

After superheroes leap, why don't they keep going up? Once they leave the ground, the only force acting on them is gravity. It pushes down on them and eventually stops them from rising. If they measure the leap correctly, they will land safely on top of the object they were jumping to.

Running at Super Speeds

When people run, they demonstrate Newton's laws of motion. The foot pushes down onto the ground at an angle, and the ground pushes back, also at an angle. Olympic sprinters can run at speeds up to 28 miles per hour (45 km/h).

Superheroes take running to new levels. Some, such as Quicksilver, can run faster than the speed of sound, which is more than 750 miles per hour (1,207 km/h). When this happens, a sonic boom occurs. Normally when people run, waves of air pressure travel in front of them like waves being pushed in front of a slow boat. At the speed of sound, the pressure waves in front of a superhero cannot move away fast enough. They build up on top of one another. The built-up waves create one big wave of pressure that makes a loud boom.

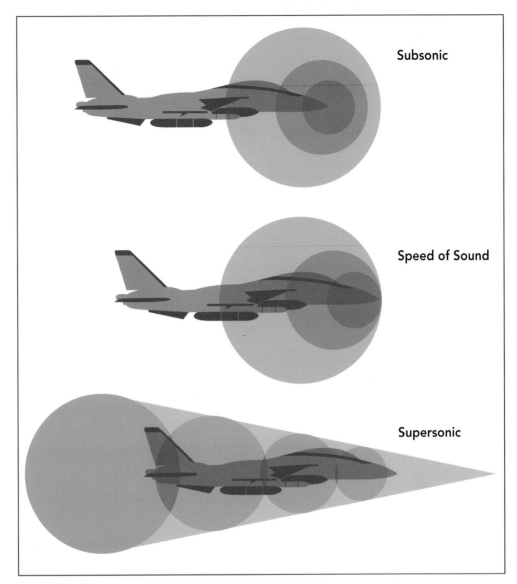

Subsonic

Speed of Sound

Supersonic

Supersonic

The diagram above shows a jet as it passes through the sound barrier. *Subsonic* means the jet is traveling slower than the speed of sound. *Supersonic* means it has surpassed the speed of sound. The circles represent pressure, or sound, waves caused by the front end of the plane. What happens to the sound waves when the plane is traveling at the speed of sound?

CHAPTER THREE

THE FOUR FORCES OF FLIGHT

In superhero stories, people are often surprised to see superheroes flying by. Citizens might mistake them for birds or planes. Like all flying things, superheroes must use the four forces that affect flight. Two of those forces, lift and thrust, support flight. Two others, gravity and drag, try to bring flying objects back to the ground. Lift is what gets something off the ground. Thrust makes the object move forward

Supergirl and Superman both have the ability to control the gravity around them, which allows them to fly.

through the air. Gravity pulls things down toward the ground. Drag works as friction slows an object down.

A Matter of Pressure

In the 1700s, scientist Daniel Bernoulli helped explain the principles behind how birds fly. The wings of birds have what is called an airfoil shape. They are curved at the top. Since the top surface is longer, air flows faster over it. This creates a lower air pressure. Air flows more slowly over the flat, shorter surface underneath the wing, making the air pressure greater. The high air pressure underneath the wings pushes the bird up through the lower air pressure. This fact is known as Bernoulli's principle. The difference in pressure is called lift. It is the force that allows the bird to take off. To create thrust, birds flap their wings. The wing pushes backward against the air, and the air pushes forward, moving the bird ahead.

An airplane's wings are shaped like those of a bird. This shape gives them lift. Thrust often comes from jet engines. Jet engines take in a lot of air. They

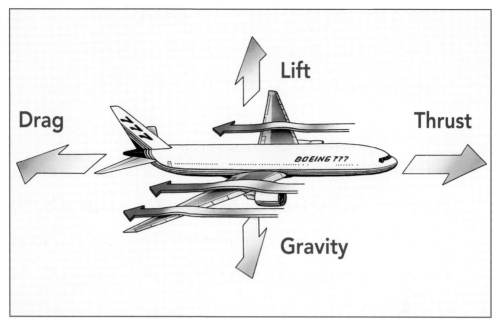

The Four Forces of Flight
The blue arrows in the diagram represent the four forces acting on an airplane. The red arrows represent the flow of air over the airfoil wings. How is the flow of air over the airfoil related to the force of the thrust?

condense the air together and heat it up by burning fuel. The dense, hot air expands and is pushed out of the back of the engine in a strong stream. The stream of air propels the plane forward. The engines must create enough thrust to overcome the force of drag and move the plane forward. The forward motion keeps the air flowing over the wings, creating lift. Lift and thrust get the plane off the ground and keep it

The superhero Falcon uses a high-tech suit with wings to achieve flight.

moving through the air. Many superheroes use wings to create lift and thrust in order to fly.

It's a Rocket!

A rocket is different from a jet. A jet engine needs air to work; a rocket does not. Rockets carry their own supplies of oxygen. They can operate in space, where there is no air. Like jets, rockets use hot, expanding gas to propel themselves. Rockets do not need airfoils. Wings help airplanes fly horizontally, but rockets launch vertically. Airfoils also create drag, which would slow a rocket down. In order to escape the pull of Earth's gravity, a rocket must fly at least 25,020 miles per hour (40,270 km/h). Drag created by airfoils would mean more thrust would be needed to get to that speed.

Iron Man flies like a rocket. He carries a reactor that creates plasma, a superhot form of gas. This fuel is then

Moving in Space

Movement in outer space works differently than movement in Earth's atmosphere. The forces of gravity and drag do not apply to objects in space. Floating in space is similar to swimming underwater. Underwater, water pushes on a person on all sides. This can make a person feel as though gravity is not present. But unlike being underwater, space has nothing to push against in order for a person to move. If someone floats even two inches (5 cm) away from a space station, there is no way to "swim" back. Astronauts use safety tethers to keep from floating off into space. If an astronaut drifts away from the surface of a station, the person can pull on the tether to return.

Iron Man can adjust the direction of his thrusters. This allows him to control his lift and thrust.

pumped down to his feet and shoots out the nozzles on his boots. This provides both lift and thrust for him to fly.

It's a Glider!

Glider flight deals with only three forces: lift, drag, and gravity. Gliders have no engines or flapping wings to give them thrust. Air is forced under the wings to oppose gravity and produce lift. Gliders move slowly down through the air. Drag slows them down until there is no more lift. Gravity pulls them back to Earth.

IN THE REAL WORLD

Flying like a Rocket

People can use water jet packs to achieve flight. A water jet pack uses the same principles as a rocket. The device uses a hose connected from a boat to the pack. Water travels up the hose and into the jet pack. It then flows through the nozzles on the jet pack at a high pressure. This gives the person lift and thrust. A 150-pound (68-kg) person can be propelled up to 22 miles per hour (25 km/h) at a height of 28 feet (8.5 m) using a water jet pack.

Batman uses his wings like a glider in order to provide lift.

Batman has no superpowers. He uses high-tech tools to help him fight crime. If he jumps from a tall building, he uses a cape to help him land safely on the ground. Like a hang-glider pilot, Batman jumps off a tall structure to get moving. The force of lift under the wings of his cape keeps him aloft as drag and gravity bring him slowly to the ground.

In the following excerpt, four physics students consider the science behind Batman using his glider cape to safely reach the ground after jumping from a tall building:

In the film Batman Begins, *Batman can glide from tall buildings using his 'memory cloth' cape, which becomes rigid when a current is passed through it. . . . Batman can glide to a distance of about 350 m [1,150 feet], which is reasonable; the problem with the glide lies in his velocity as he reaches ground level. The velocity rises rapidly to a maximum of a little over 110 km/h [68 mph] before steadying to a constant speed of around 80 km/h [50 mph]. At these high speeds any impact would likely be fatal if not severely damaging (consider impact with a car travelling at these speeds).*

Source: D. A. Marshall, T. O. Hands, I. Griffiths, and G. Douglas. "Trajectory of a Falling Batman." Journal of Physics Special Topics 10.1 (2011): A2_9. December 9, 2011. Web. January 20, 2016.

Back It Up

These authors are using evidence to support a point. Write a paragraph describing the point the authors are making. Then write down two pieces of evidence the authors use to make their point.

CHAPTER FOUR

CHANGING WEATHER

Storm is a superhero with a mutation that gives her the power to control weather. She does this by changing the air temperature at will. Whenever she wants to, she can create hurricanes, tornadoes, and blizzards. Then she can undo it all and make the skies clear.

Weather is caused by differences in temperature between large pockets of air. Gases and dust particles

Storm can create extreme weather conditions at a moment's notice.

Mountains Control Their Own Weather

Tall mountains, like some superheroes, can create their own weather. As air masses move toward mountains, the air gets forced upward. Water droplets condense, forming clouds. The clouds drop rain, sleet, or snow on the windward side of the mountains. The air mass moves over the top of the mountains. Mountains force air masses upward. Here the air cools quickly. It dries out as the precipitation falls out of it. The air also warms quickly as it moves toward a lower elevation. This is why the leeward side of mountain ranges are mostly dry and warm.

in Earth's atmosphere absorb some of the energy from the sun. But more of the sun's energy passes through the atmosphere and is absorbed by Earth's surface. The air near the ground warms, and then it rises and meets cooler air high up in the atmosphere. The cooler temperature causes condensation. Water droplets form around the dust particles floating in the air. The droplets cling together. This cooler air becomes more dense, and water falls to the ground.

After a while, the air warms. It again rises and cools. This is a continuous cycle called thermal convection.

Storm's mutations give her the power to change the air temperature at will. She can cause convection currents in the air around her. The warm air rises and forms clouds. The droplets in the clouds become too heavy. They fall to the ground as precipitation. This is how she creates thunderstorms.

Rain, Hail, Sleet, or Snow?

Iceman is another superhero who can control temperature. He is able to lower the temperature of his body, forming a protective coating of ice. He can also project waves of coldness and turn water vapor to ice.

Temperature determines what type of precipitation falls to the ground. If the temperature of the precipitation is 32 degrees Fahrenheit (0°C) or colder, it will fall as snow, sleet, or hail. Hail is made up of large frozen raindrops. Hail is produced when precipitation freezes during a thunderstorm. As it

Iceman, *left*, can control the temperature of the air around him and turn water vapor into ice.

falls, strong updrafts from the thunderstorm bring the frozen precipitation back upward, where it collects more water. This cycle repeats itself until the hail is too heavy to be lifted in the updraft. It then falls to the ground as balls of ice.

Sleet is made up of frozen raindrops that start out as snow. The droplets fall through pockets of warm and cold air. They thaw in the warm air and then freeze again in the cold air. They hit the ground as small ice pellets.

Snowflakes are formed in the cold air of a cloud. Ice crystals slowly freeze around dust particles. If the air at ground level is also cold, the snowflakes pile up. Ordinary people shape piles of snow into snowmen and other figures. Similarly, Iceman can form the ice he makes into any object he chooses. He has created ladders, shields, and slides to help him escape his enemies.

FURTHER EVIDENCE

Chapter Four covers different types of precipitation. What was one of the main points of this chapter? What evidence is included to support this point? Read the article at the website below. Does the information support the main point of the chapter? What new information is presented in the article?

Winter Storms

mycorelibrary.com/science-of-superheroes

HEALING AND ADRENALINE

Superheroes thrive in extreme situations. Wolverine has a mutation called a healing factor. If he becomes injured, his healing factor allows him to recover incredibly quickly. Hulk also responds well to intense situations. When he gets angry, adrenaline pumps through his body. The madder he gets, the stronger he becomes. The adrenaline pulsing through his body gives his

The more upset Hulk gets, the stronger he becomes.

Wolverine's claws break through his skin every time he takes them out, but the skin quickly heals after he puts them away.

muscles the ability to perform unbelievable feats. Humans cannot recover from gunshot wounds in minutes like Wolverine or lift mountains like Hulk. But the human body can recover quickly from injury and use adrenaline to excel under stress.

Good as New

Human bodies repair wounds such as cuts in four stages. First blood vessels close to the wound tighten. This reduces the flow of blood. Sticky blood cells called platelets clump together. They form a plug for the hole in the blood vessel. The bleeding stops. Next blood vessels become larger. They deliver white blood cells to the wound. These cells go to work destroying germs. The skin swells in the area of the cut. This stage of the process is called inflammation.

Once the germs are destroyed, the process of repair begins. Special skin cells produce collagen. This is a protein found in skin and bones. The collagen fills in the skin. It makes new blood vessels to deliver oxygen. The new tissue stretches to meet the skin at the other side of the cut. A scar forms. Over time the new tissue becomes stronger. Eventually it will be almost as strong as it was before the wound occurred.

Sometimes our bodies encounter more serious traumas, such as deep wounds or burns. These require

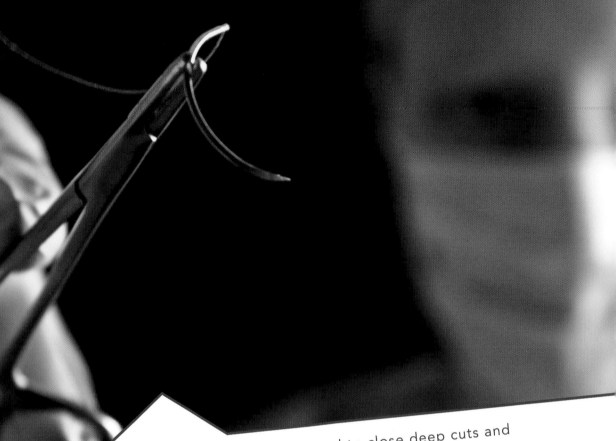

Doctors use needle and thread to close deep cuts and help the body heal.

visits to the doctor. Doctors can help by stitching skin together, making it easier for the skin to reconnect. If a person has a large burn, doctors can make a skin graft over the wound. They remove a patch of healthy skin from one part of the body and stitch it to the wounded area. In time the area looks normal, although there may be a slight scar. These procedures help large or deep wounds heal more quickly and have less scarring than they would if they had healed on their own.

Superhuman Strength

Many superheroes do not have healing factors. They rely on other powers to get them through tough situations. Like Hulk, Captain America uses super strength. A special chemical changed his body to operate at peak human performance. Not only does he have great strength, but he also has excellent endurance and reflexes. Normal humans do not have these superhero traits, but we do have

New Way to Help Burns Heal

Severe burns can leave scars on a person for the rest of his or her life. But doctors have an effective method for helping burns heal. A burn victim is put to sleep. Doctors shave off the burned flesh until they uncover healthy skin. Then they patch it with a skin substitute made from animal tissue. After two weeks, new blood vessels grow up through the patch. This creates a new layer of live skin. Doctors then apply a thin layer of the patient's own skin over it to complete the patch.

Captain America uses enhanced strength, speed, and reflexes to handle difficult situations.

adrenaline that can give us boosts in extreme situations.

When humans become excited or frightened, a signal is sent to the brain. The brain then sends the signal on to the kidneys. Special glands above the kidneys release adrenaline. The chemical enters the bloodstream. It is carried around to different cells, causing parts of the body to react.

Adrenaline increases the heart rate. The blood vessels around the heart open. This allows more

IN THE REAL WORLD

Humans into Superheroes

In 2006 in Tucson, Arizona, a man witnessed a car hit a young boy and pin him underneath. The man rushed over and lifted the car off the boy. The boy was saved. In 1982 in Lawrenceville, Georgia, a car fell off its supports onto a man working underneath the vehicle. The man's mother lifted the car up so two neighbors could replace the supports. These people were able to do these super feats because of the effects of adrenaline. The chemical helped them to become stronger for short periods of time in order to save lives.

blood to be pumped to other parts of the body. The blood carries oxygen and nutrients to muscles. The muscles are able to produce more force for longer periods of time. Extra oxygen is carried to the brain to make the person more alert and aware. Adrenaline also tightens blood veins. This slows the blood flow back to the heart. The blood stays longer in the muscles to keep them strong. These effects of adrenaline help humans to become almost superhuman.

Learning from Superheroes

People may never be able to do the amazing feats of superheroes on their own. But by studying science, people can learn about the way the world works. This can help us better understand how superheroes do what they do. It may also help people create ways to achieve the unbelievable.

In the following excerpt, researcher Jarrod James explains how adrenaline affects humans differently:

> *An adrenaline rush can affect everyone, especially college students who seem to always be under some type of physical, mental, or social stress. An adrenaline rush can take the form of anxiousness, nervousness, or a euphoric excitement in anticipation for some long-awaited, or long-dreaded, event. In students, it can be felt minutes before taking a major test, or in excitement watching the end of a close college football game. An adrenaline rush synchronizes the mind and body to take on the stresses of the outside world. To some, it is a welcomed tension; to others it is an agonizing sensation. In its purest effect, it leaves an individual thinking either one of two things, "I'm ready for this," or "I don't want to be here anymore."*

> Source: Jarrod James. "Animal Instincts of the Human Body: A Psychological and Skeletal Muscular Analysis of Adrenaline on the Human Body." The PIT Journal. University of North Carolina, 2012. Web. Accessed November 3, 2015.

What's the Big Idea?

Take a close look at this passage. What can cause an adrenaline rush? How do different people react to them?

FAST FACTS

- Superhero stories often take real scientific theories and laws and add fantasy elements.
- Isaac Newton discovered three laws of motion that explain how people and objects move.
- As someone or something breaks the speed of sound, pressure waves build up, causing a sonic boom.
- Four forces affect flight: lift, thrust, drag, and gravity.
- Wings shaped like airfoils create higher pressure underneath the wings, creating lift.
- Jet engines suck in air and push out hot, high-pressure gasses in order to create thrust.
- Rockets that travel in space carry their own supply of oxygen for their engines to work.
- Gliders use wings to create lift, but gliders do not provide thrust.
- Weather is controlled by convection, or temperature changes, within the atmosphere.

- Different types of precipitation fall at different temperatures.
- Humans do not have healing factors like Wolverine, but doctors have methods of increasing the speed of healing for injured patients.
- Humans heal in four stages: clotting, inflammation, repair, and scarring.
- When frightened or under stress, our bodies release adrenaline, a chemical that makes us stronger and more aware.

STOP AND THINK

Take a Stand

The Science and Entertainment Exchange helps those who make movies and TV shows incorporate accurate science. Do you think it is important that shows and movies show real scientific processes? Why or why not? Support your answer with an example from a show or movie you have seen.

You Are There

Chapter Five tells about how the body heals after it is wounded. Imagine you could travel inside someone's body just after an injury, such as scraping a knee. Write a journal entry telling about what you see and feel. Be sure to add plenty of details about your observations.

Dig Deeper

After reading this book, what questions do you still have about how things fly? With an adult's help, find a few reliable sources that can help you answer your questions. Write a paragraph about what you learned.

Surprise Me

Chapter Four discusses factors that cause different kinds of weather. After reading the chapter, what two or three facts about the weather did you find most surprising? Write a few sentences about each fact. Why did you find each surprising?

GLOSSARY

airfoil
a wing or blade designed to create a force when it moves through air

atmosphere
the mass of gasses that surrounds Earth

condense
to change from gas to liquid

convection
heat transfer within the atmosphere

leeward
the side that is sheltered from the wind

mutation
a change in one's genes

precipitation
water that falls to the ground

tether
a rope or strap attached to objects at both ends

thermal
relating to heat

windward
the side that the wind is blowing from

LEARN MORE

Books

Nahum, Andrew. *Flight*. New York: DK, 2011.

Simon, Seymour. *Weather*. New York: HarperCollins, 2006.

Super Heroes Storybook Collection. New York: Marvel, 2013.

Websites

To learn more about Super-Awesome Science, visit **booklinks.abdopublishing.com**. These links are routinely monitored and updated to provide the most current information available.

Visit **mycorelibrary.com** for free additional tools for teachers and students.

INDEX

ABOUT THE AUTHOR

Patricia Hutchison grew up reading Superman comics and watching Batman on TV. She was a teacher for many years. She now teaches about science through her writing. When she is not writing, she likes to travel with her husband. She loves to visit science and nature museums everywhere they go.